Efly the Elephant

Coloring Book

Janie Jones

ISBN: 9798737590291

DEDICATION

TO YOU!

BE CREATIVE!

BE BOLD!

BE UNIQUE!

BE YOU!

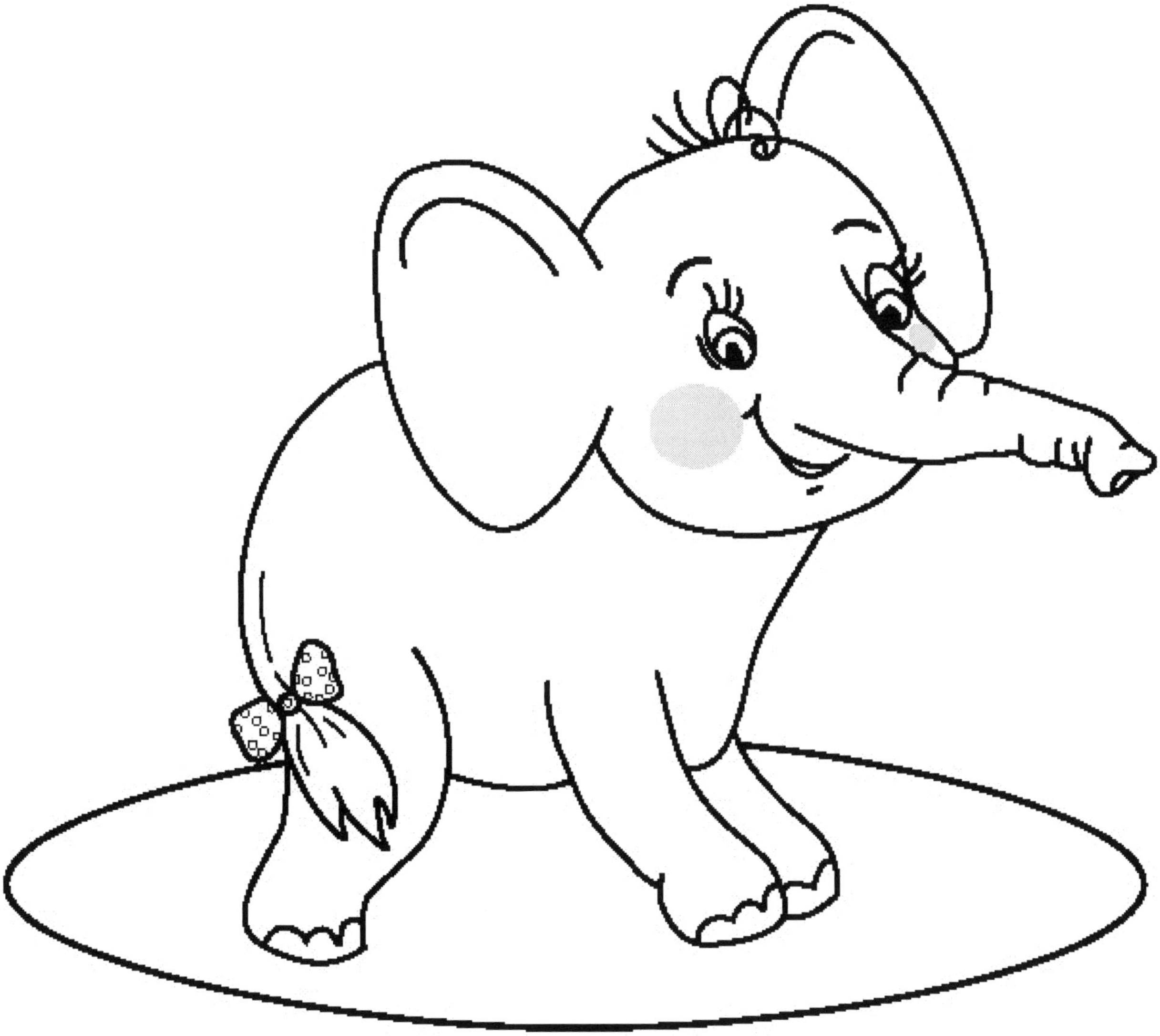

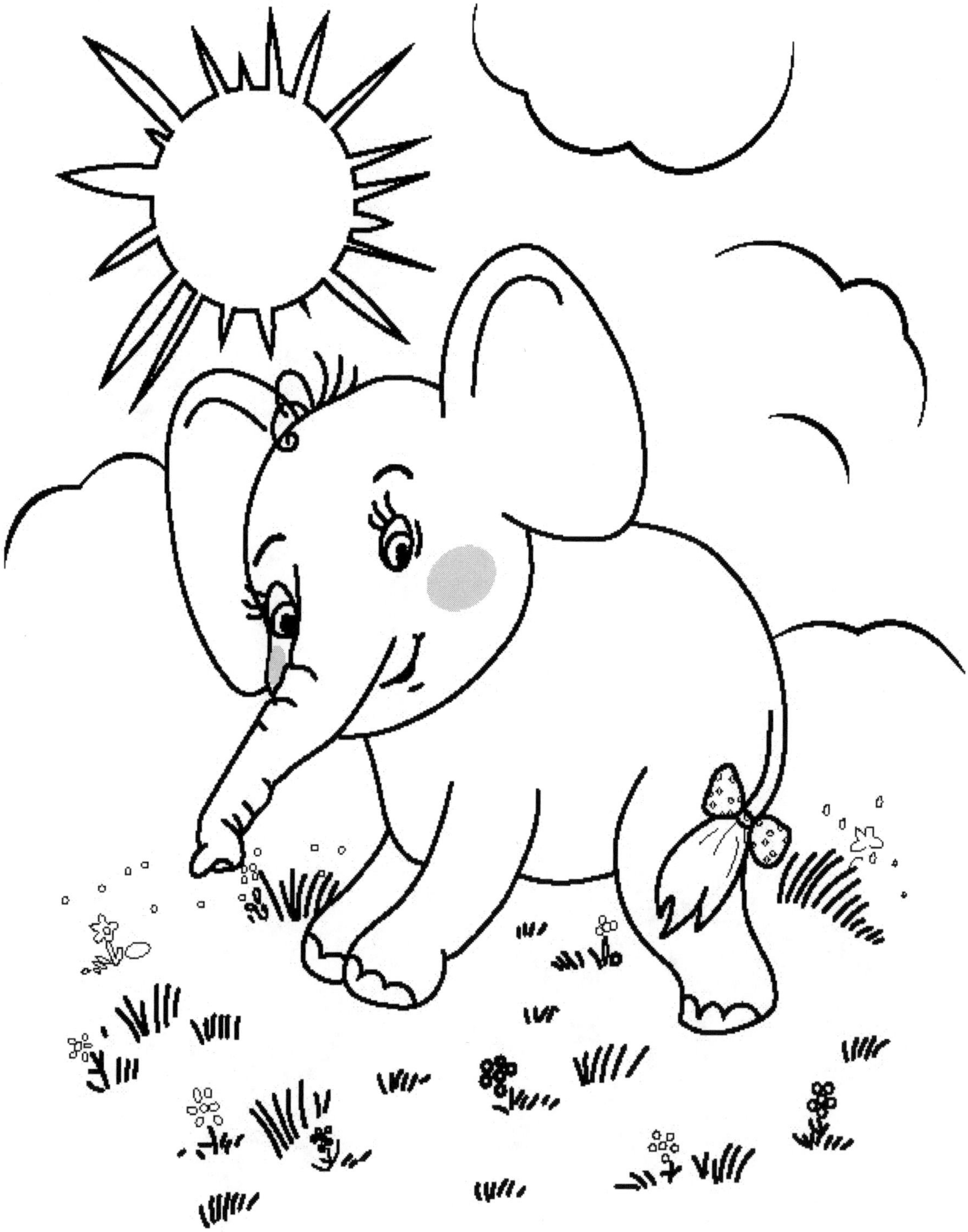

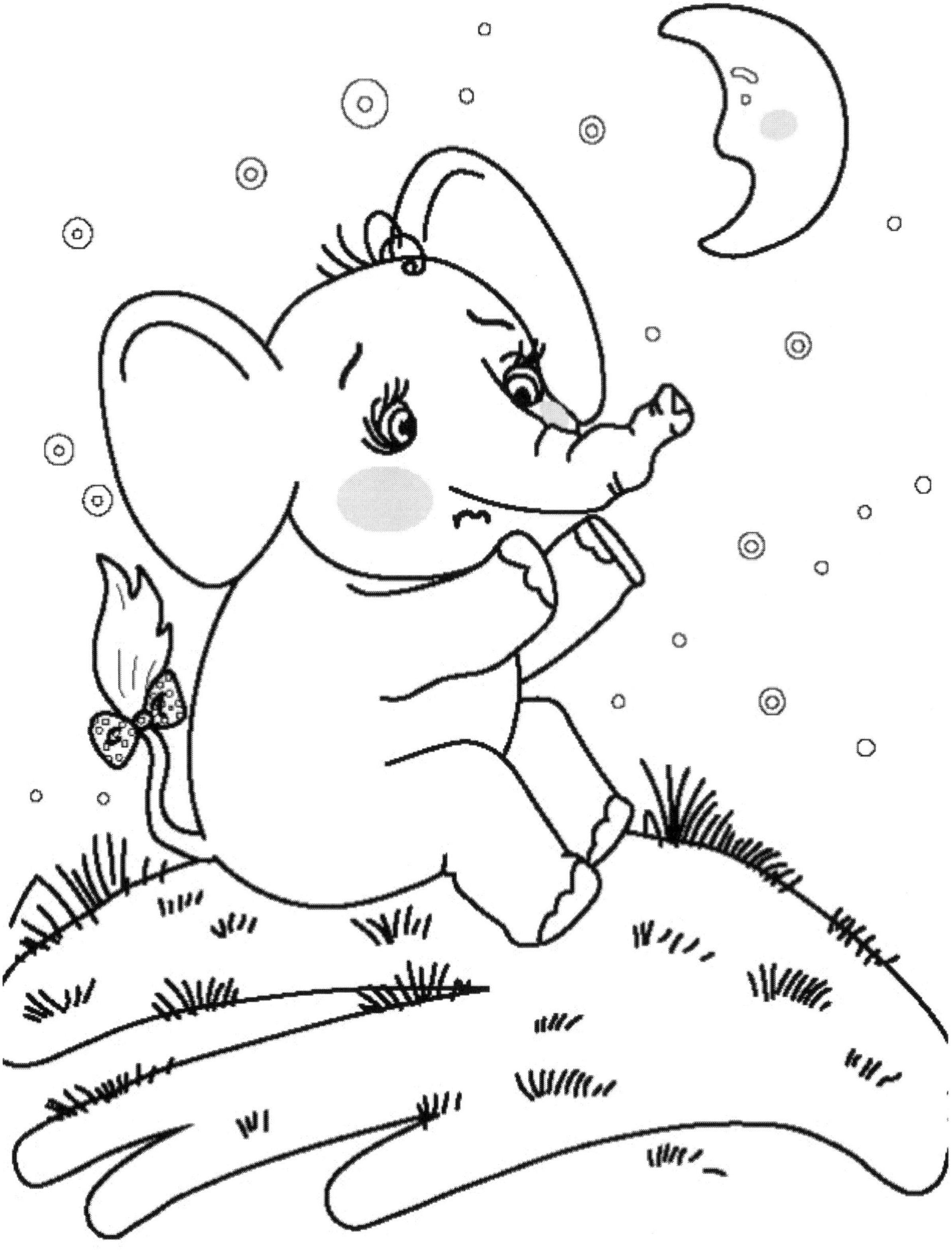

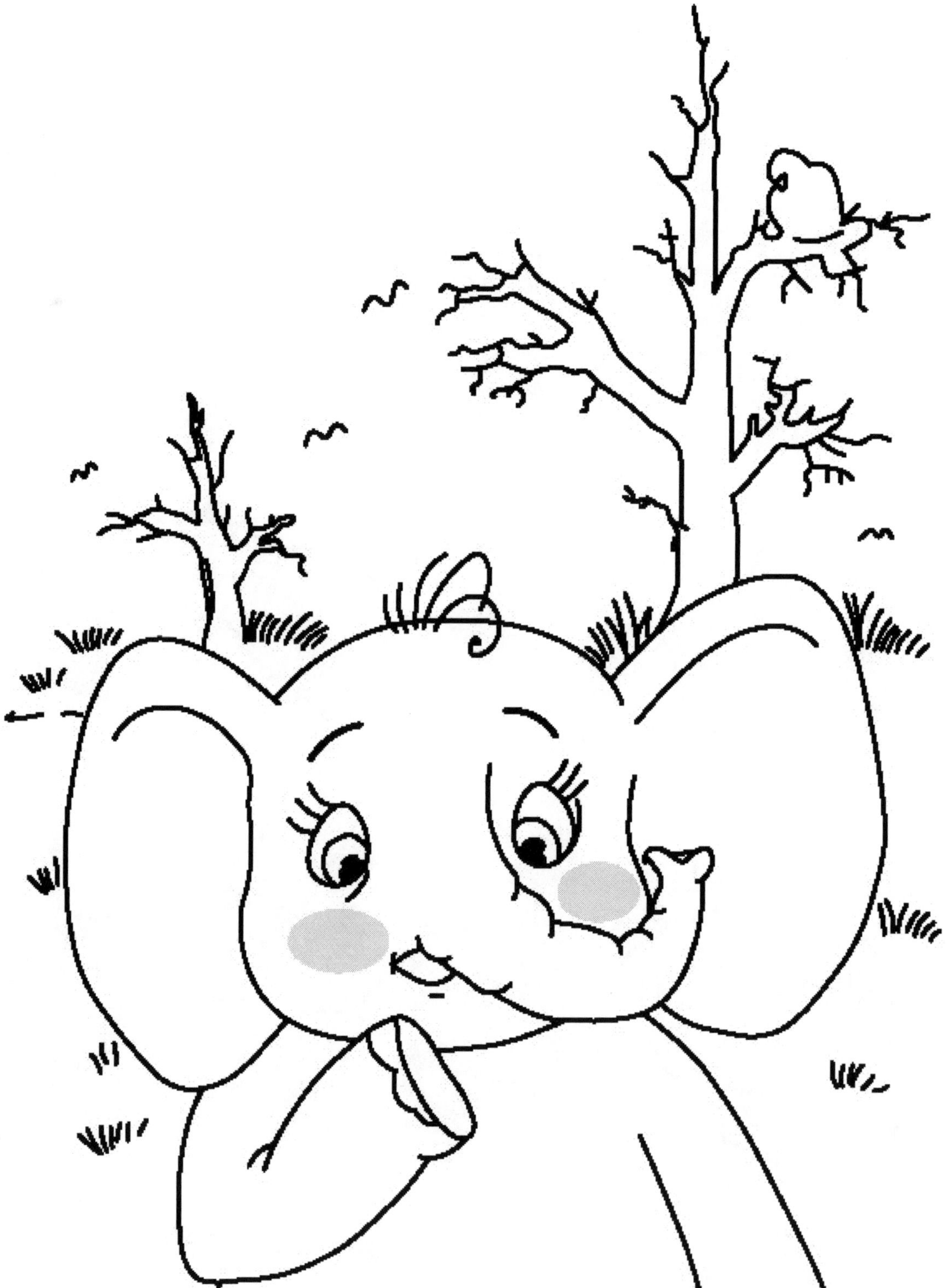

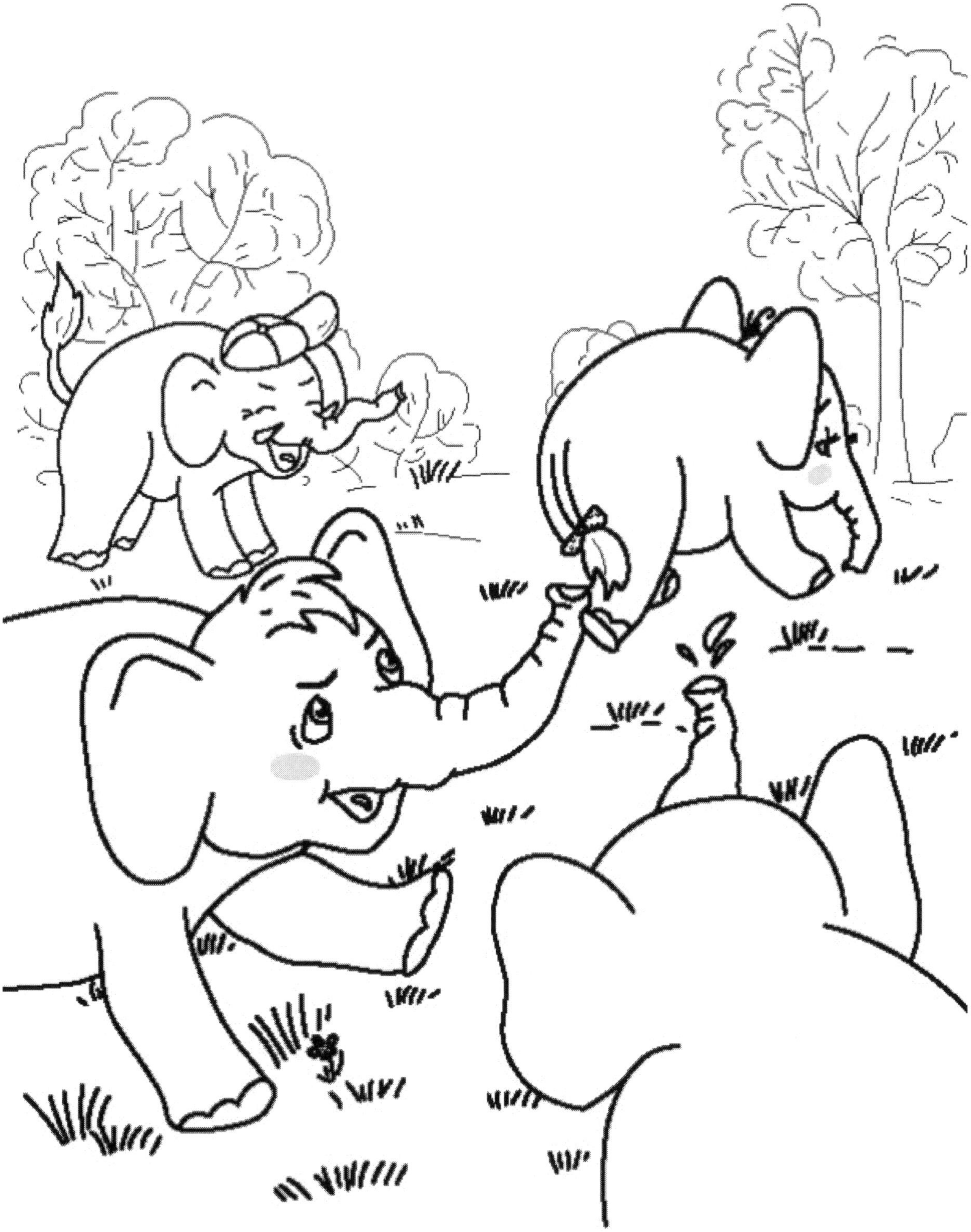

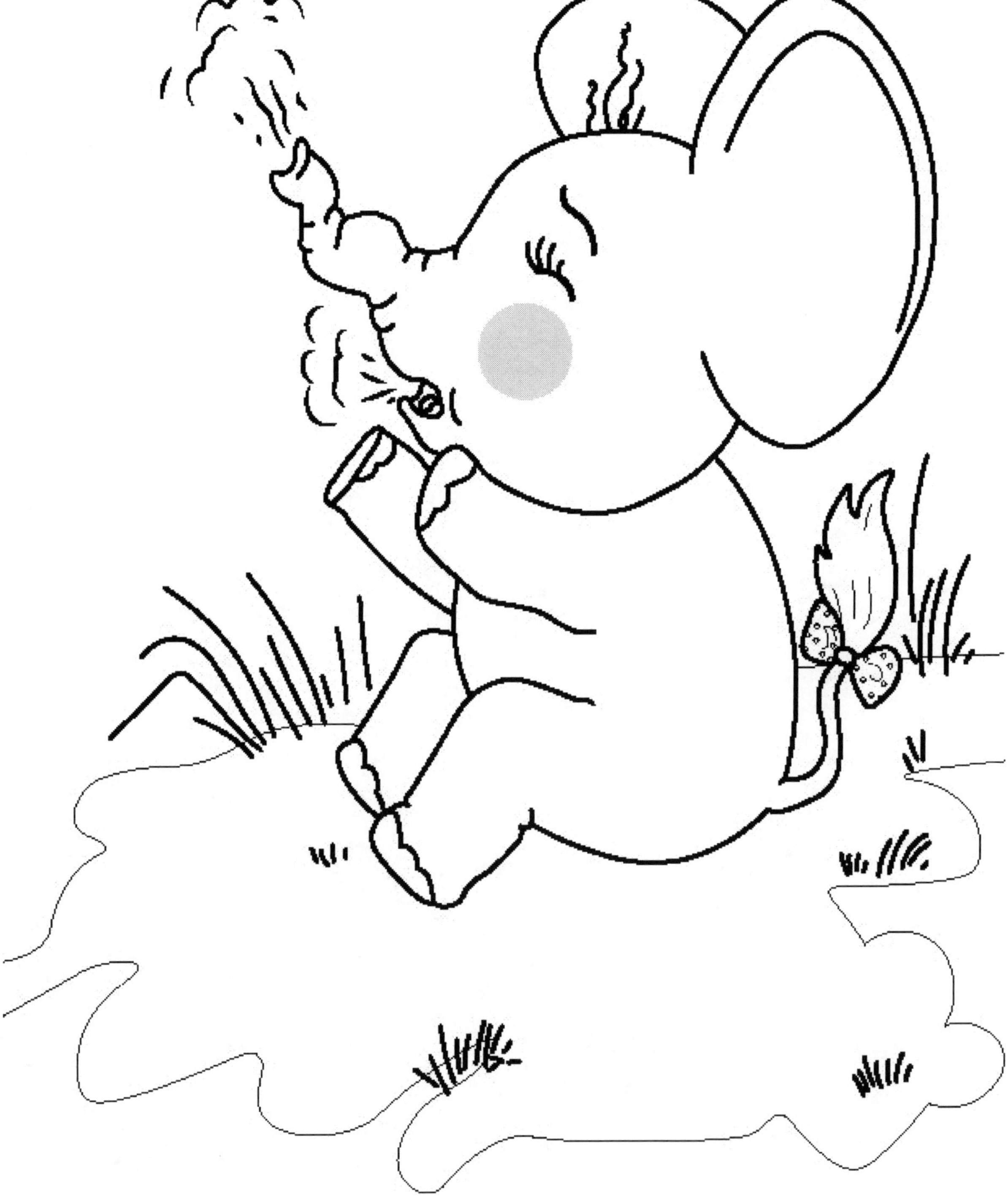

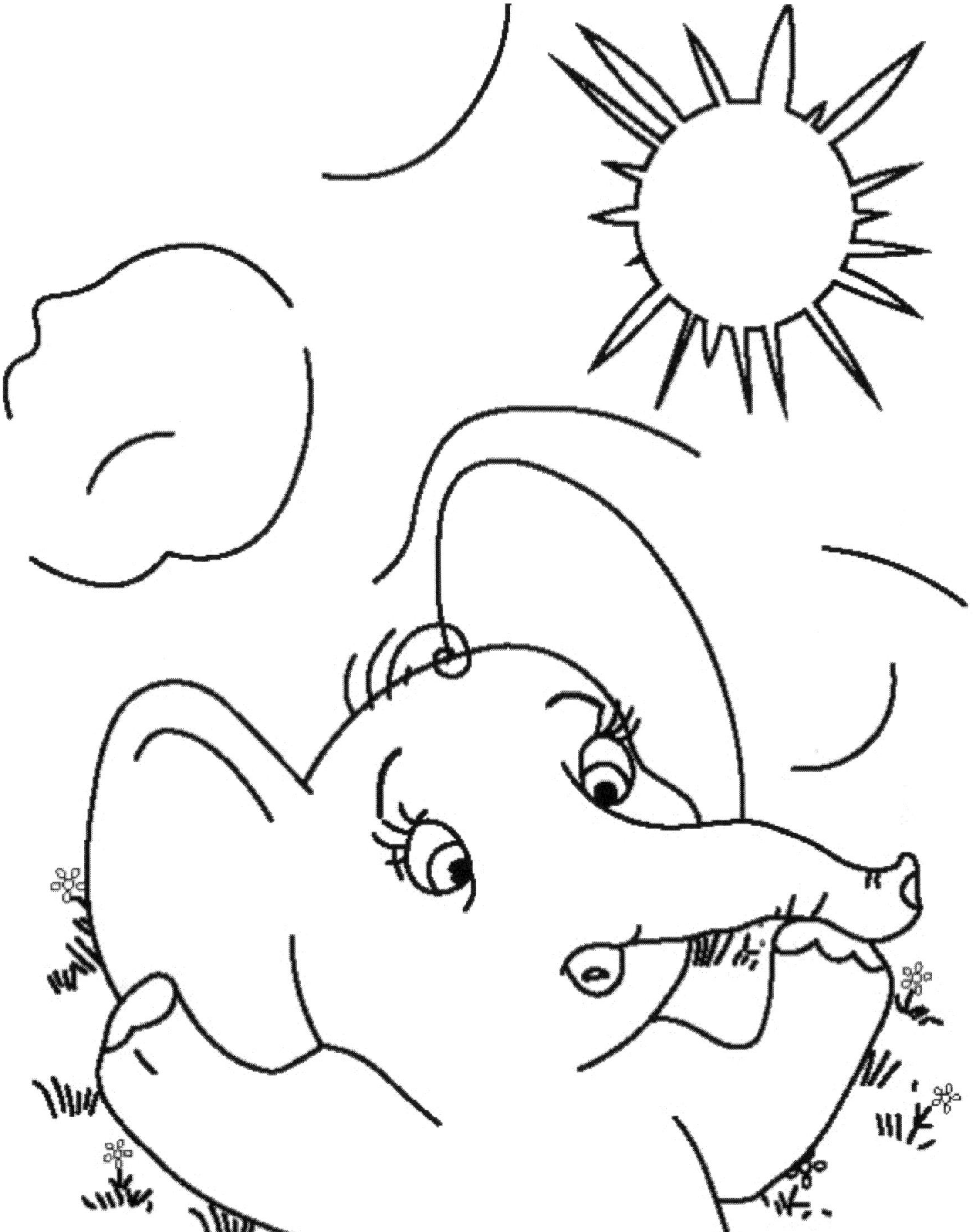

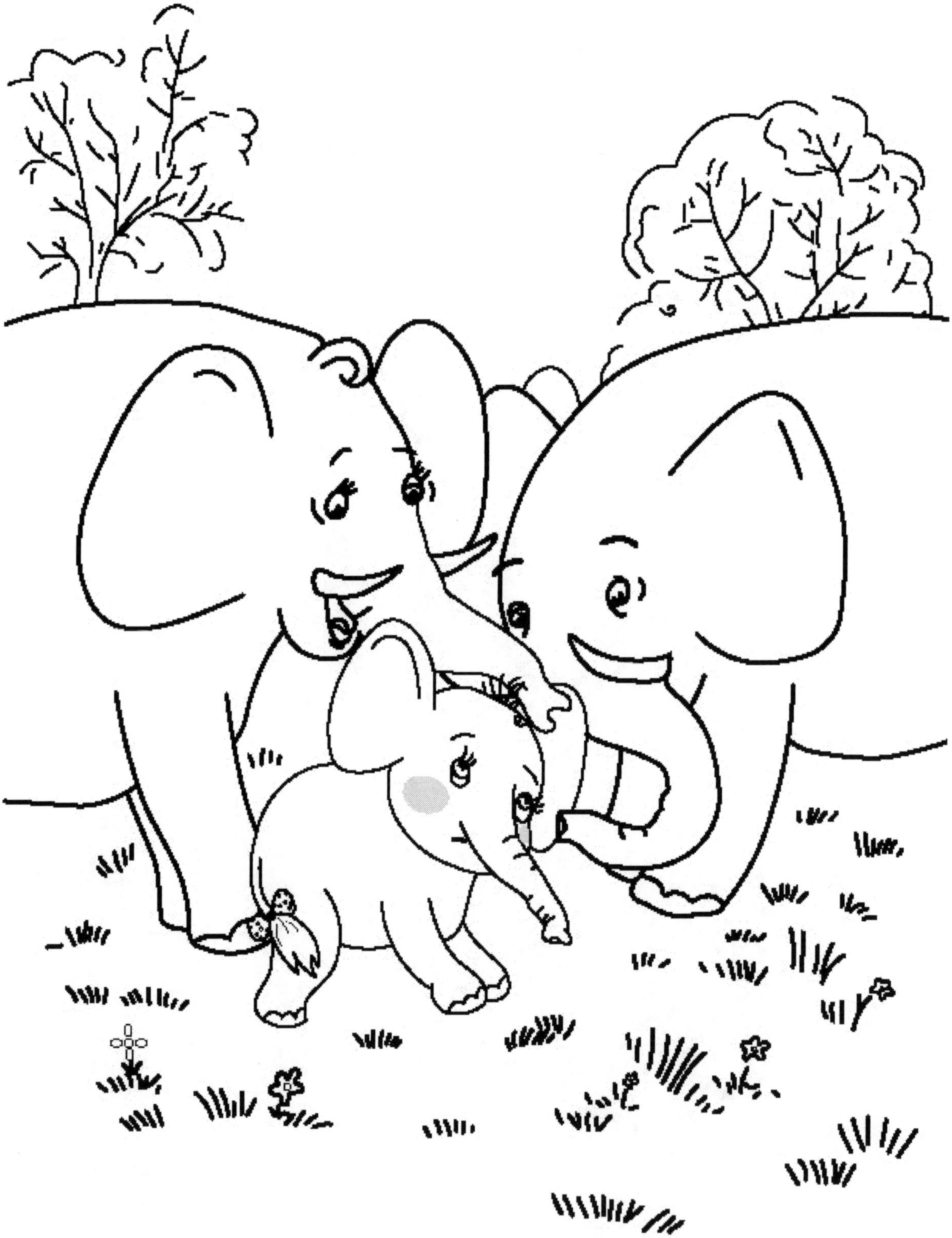

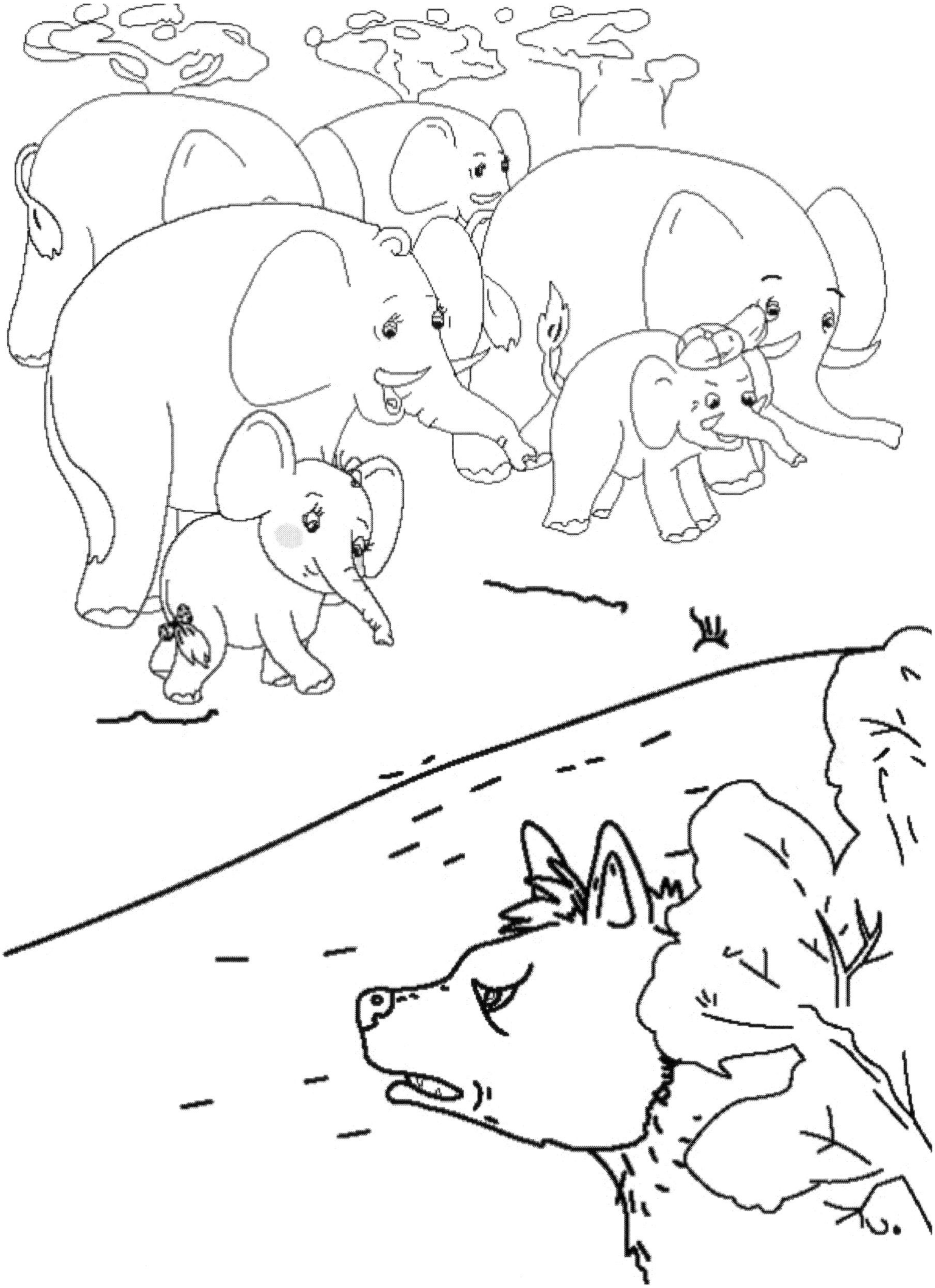

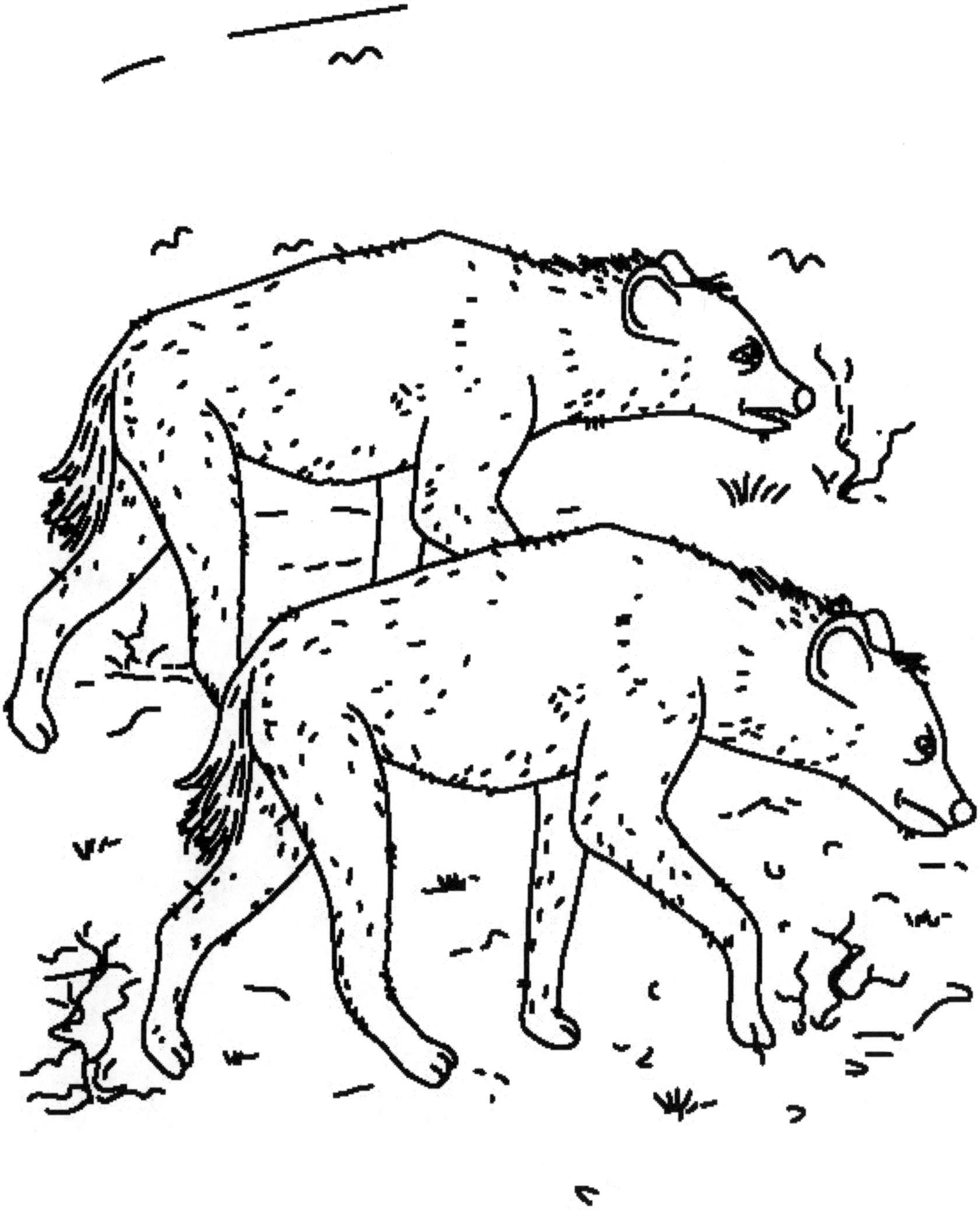

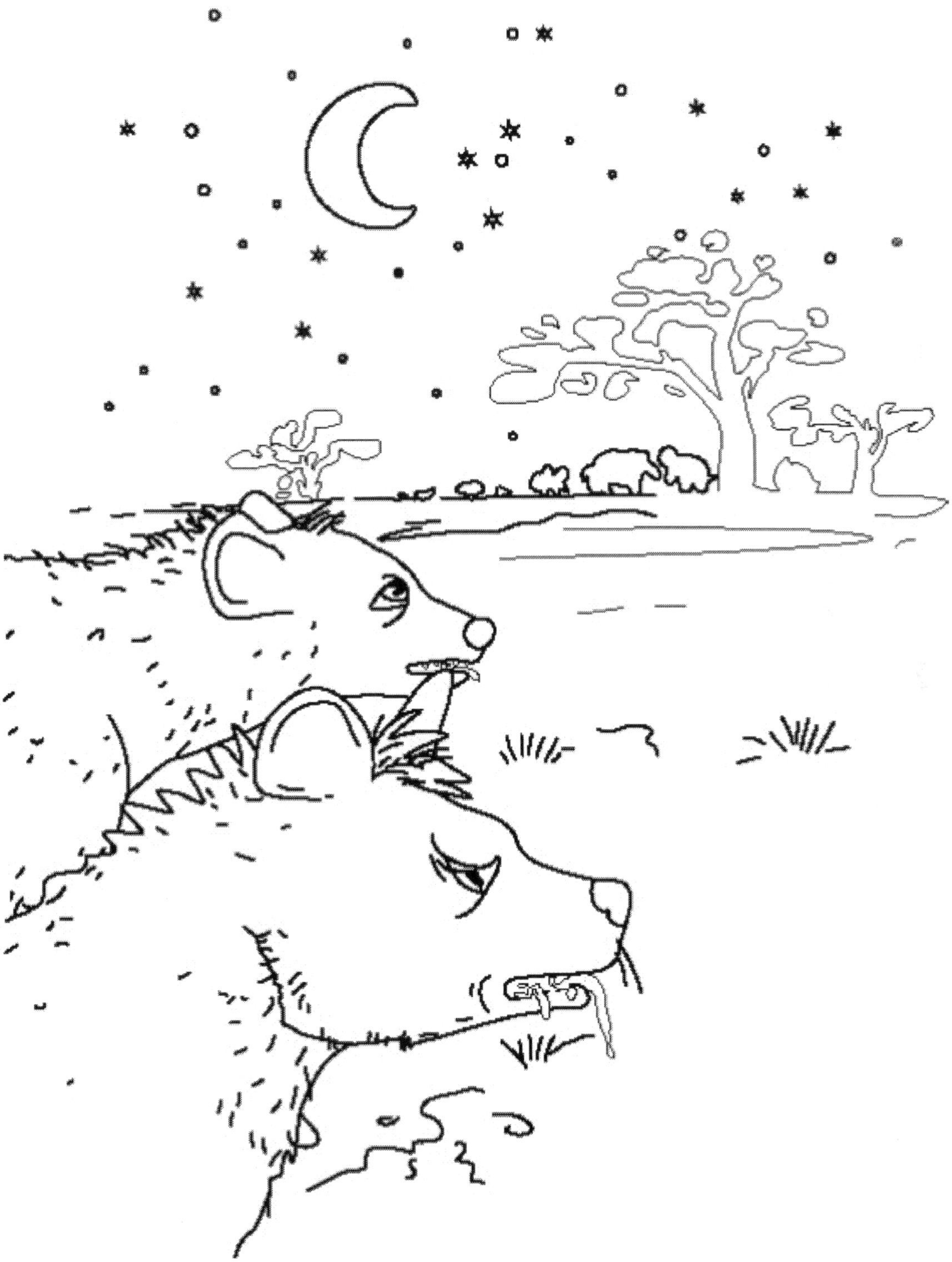

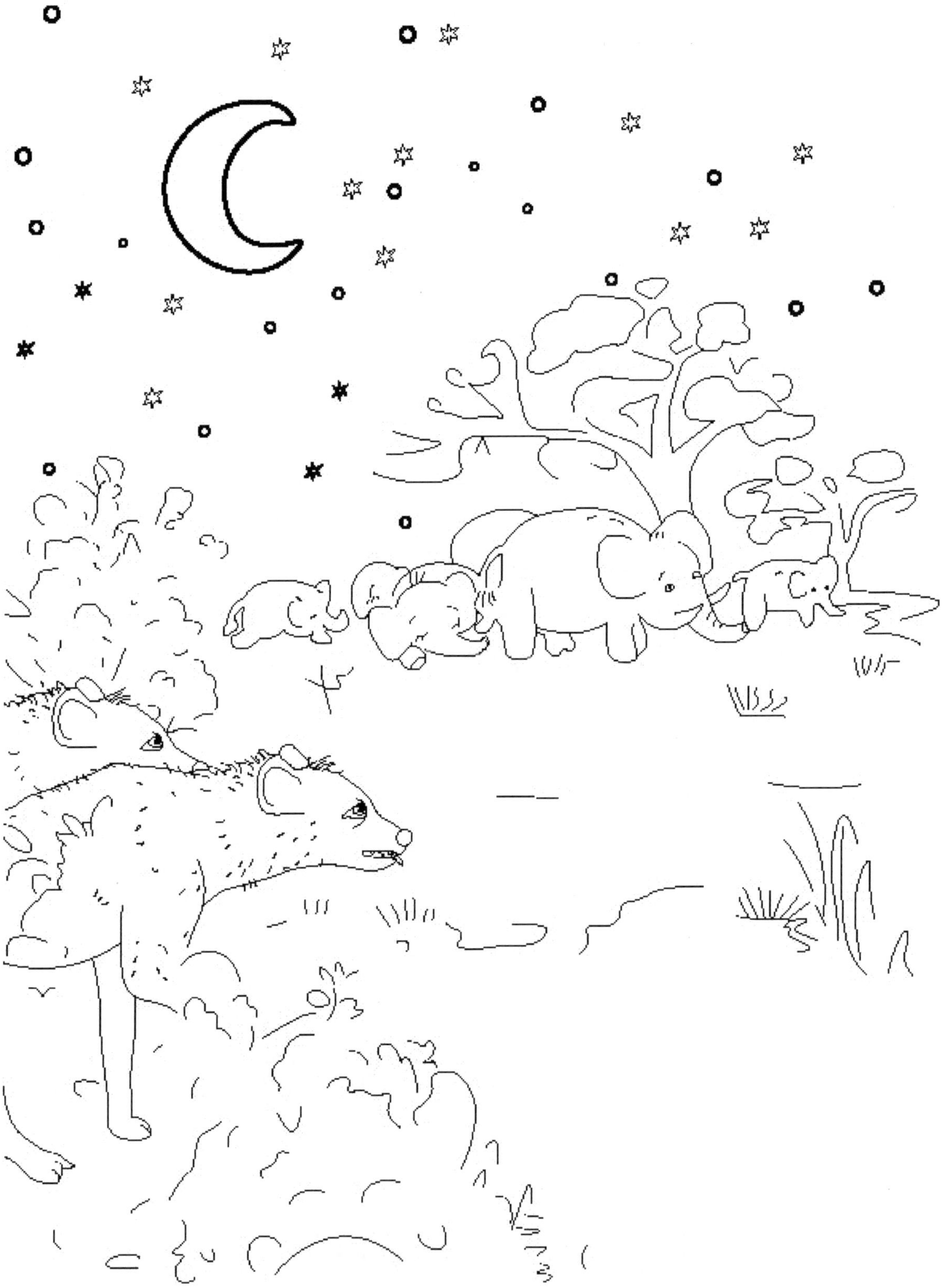

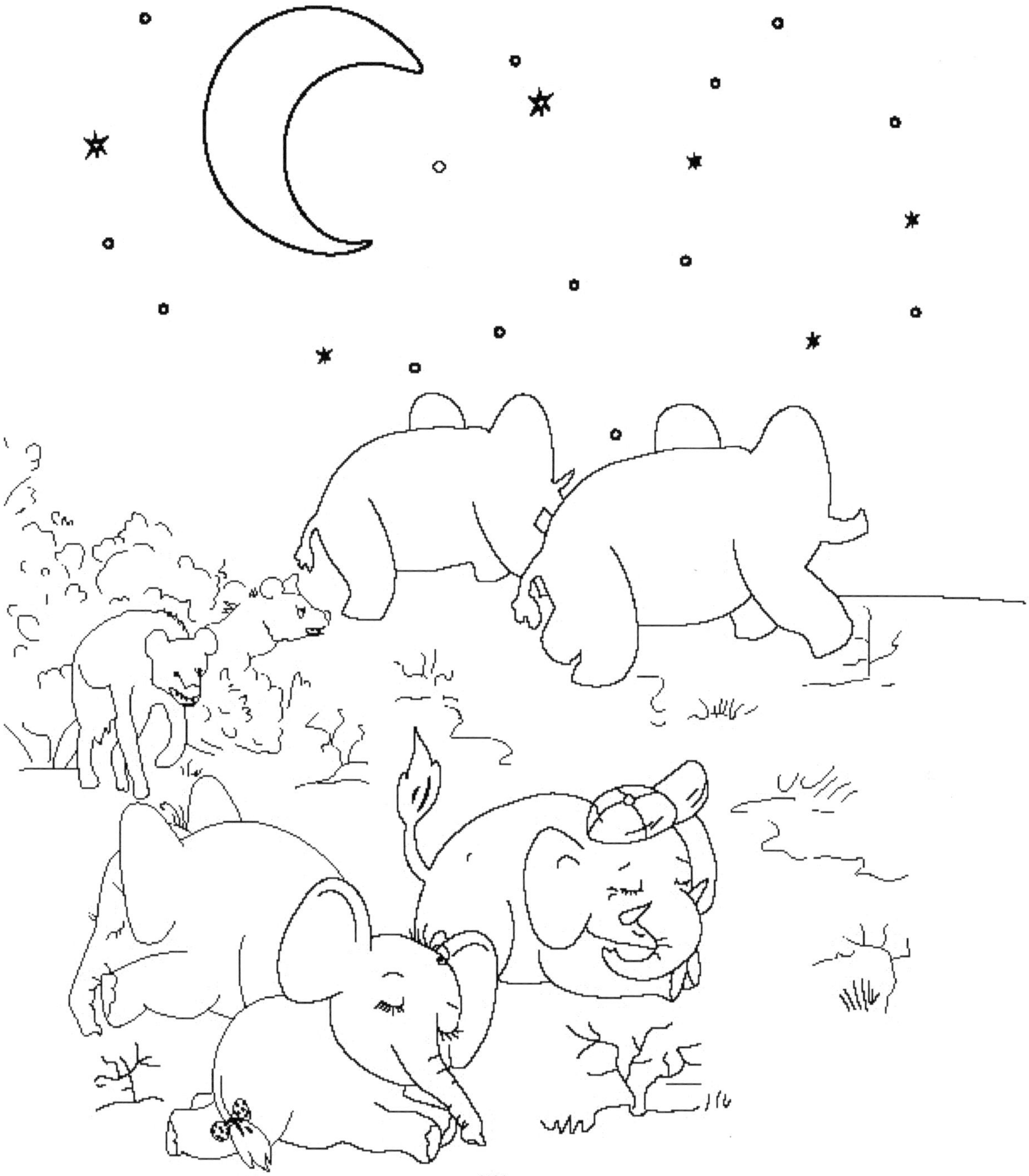

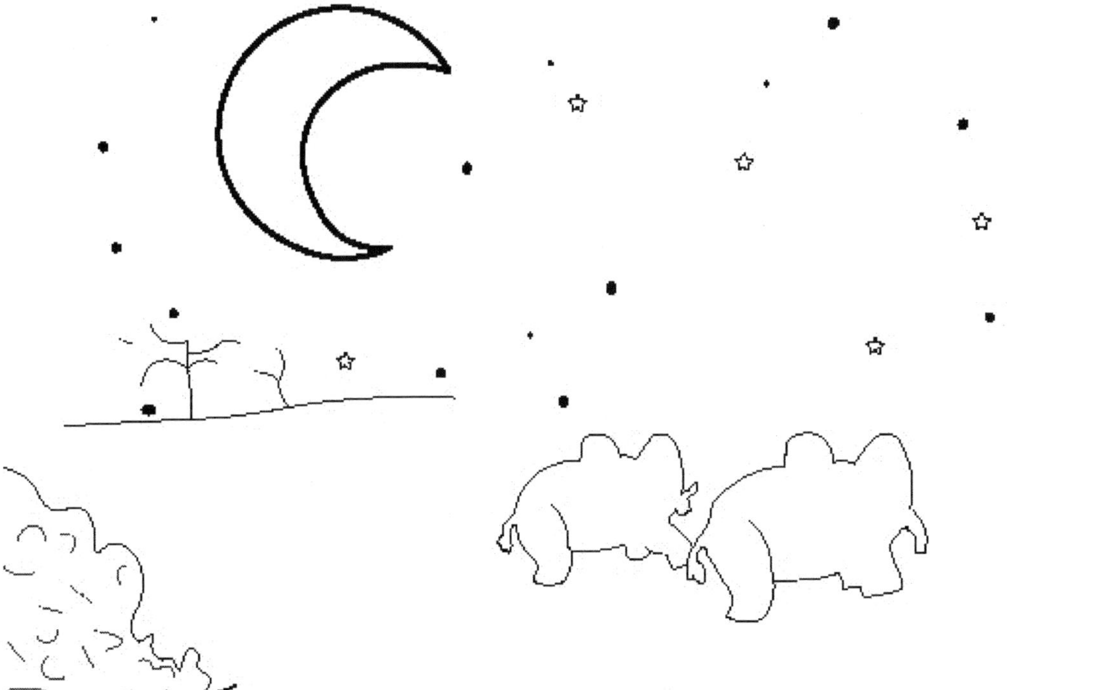

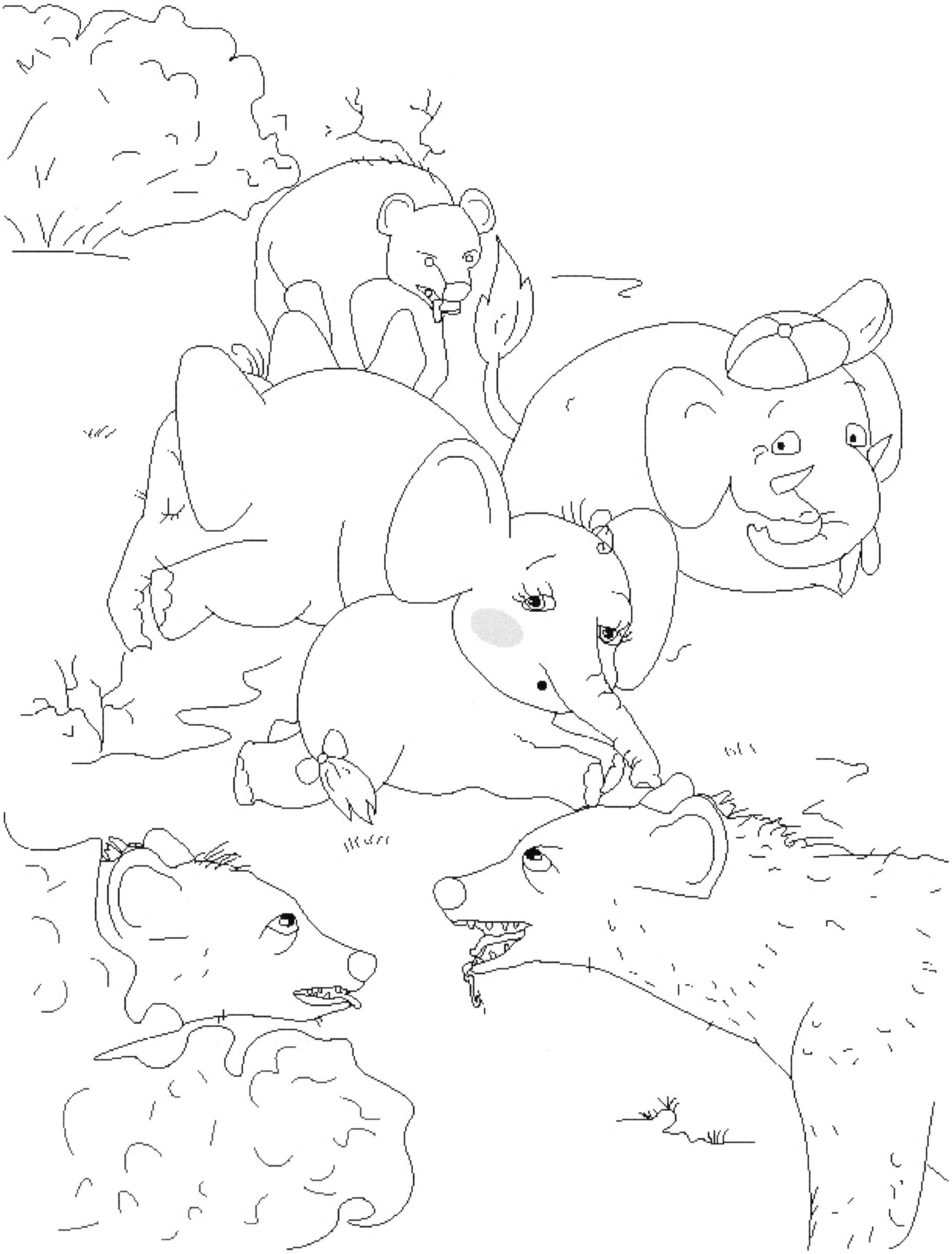

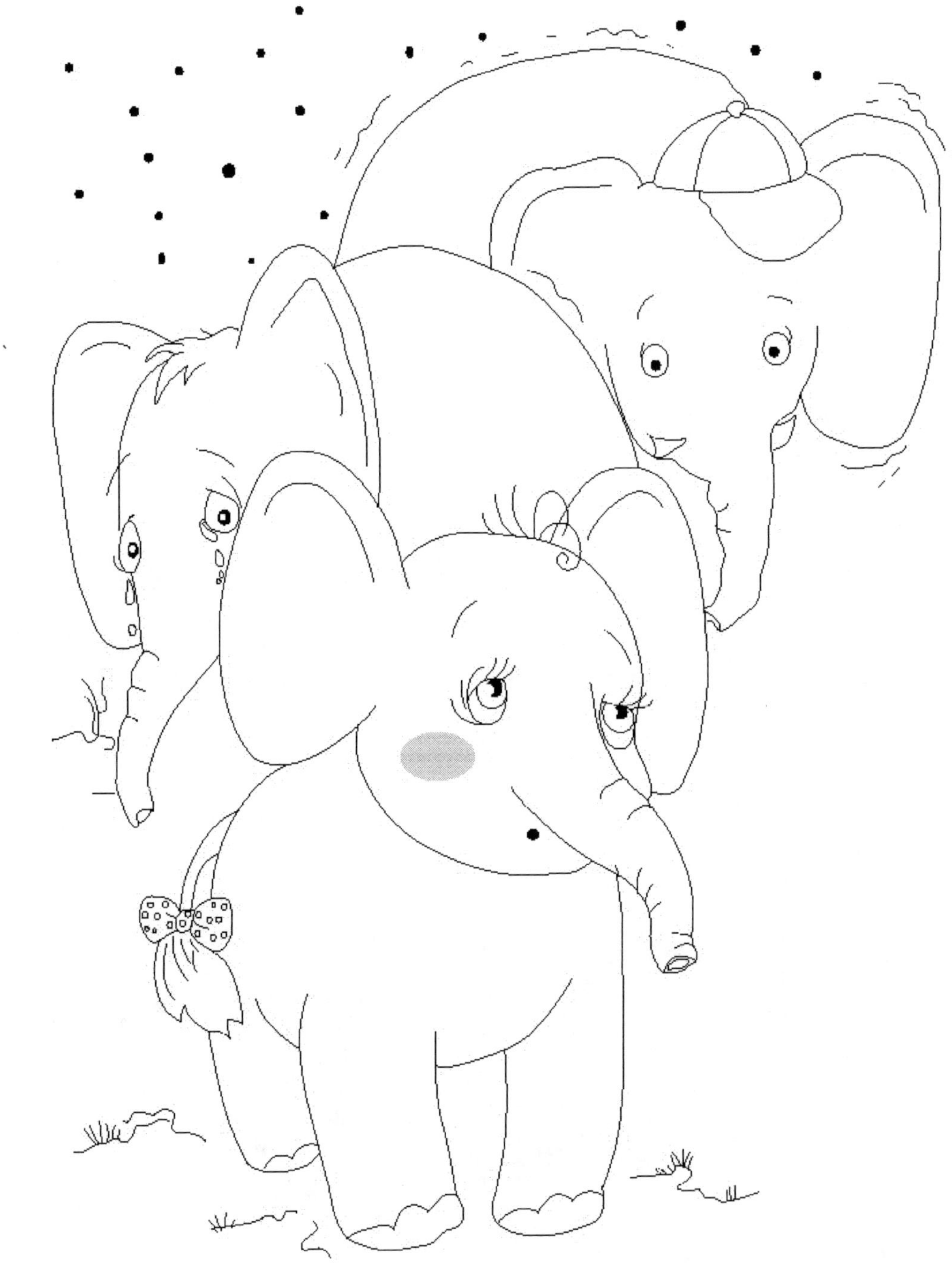

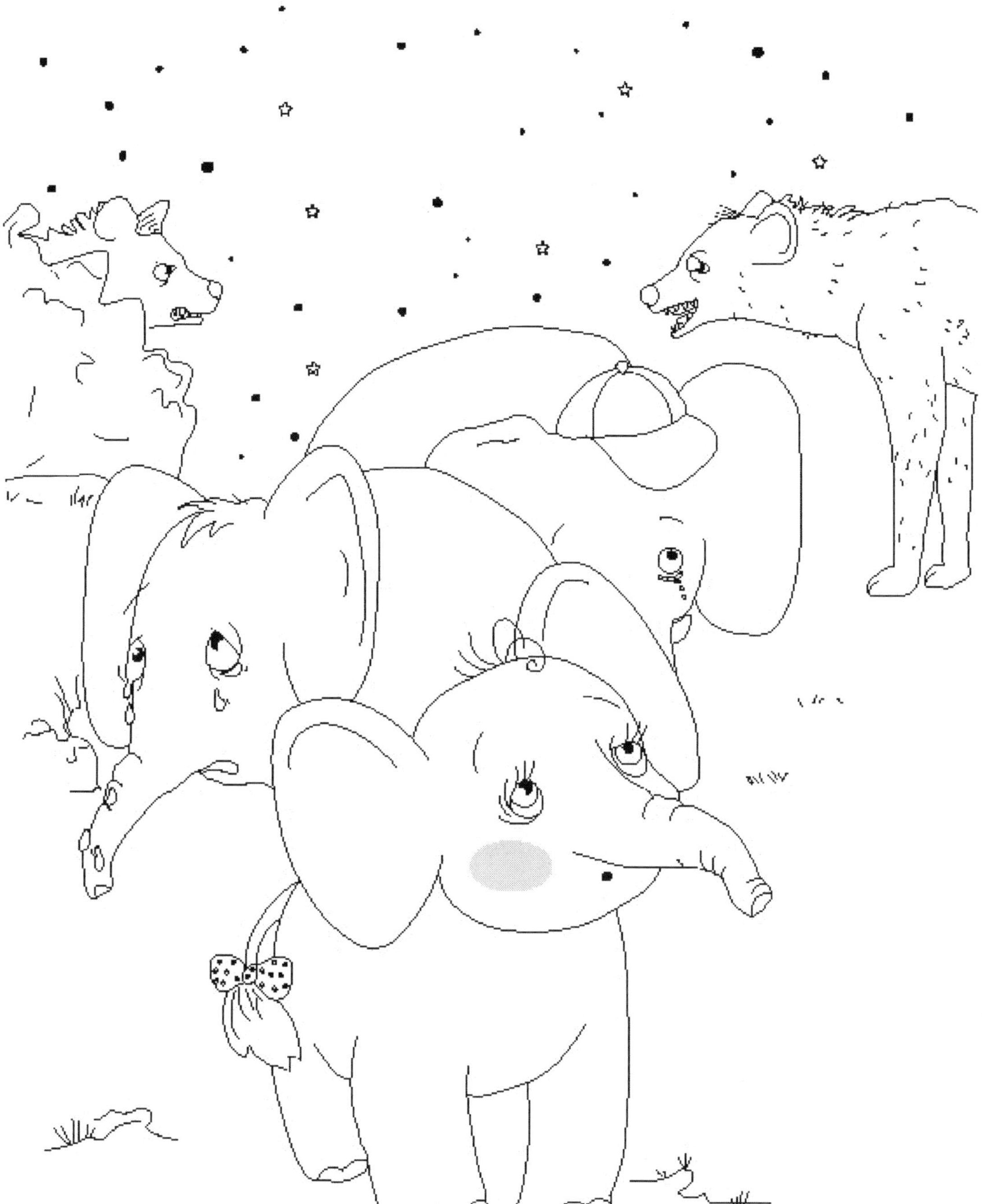

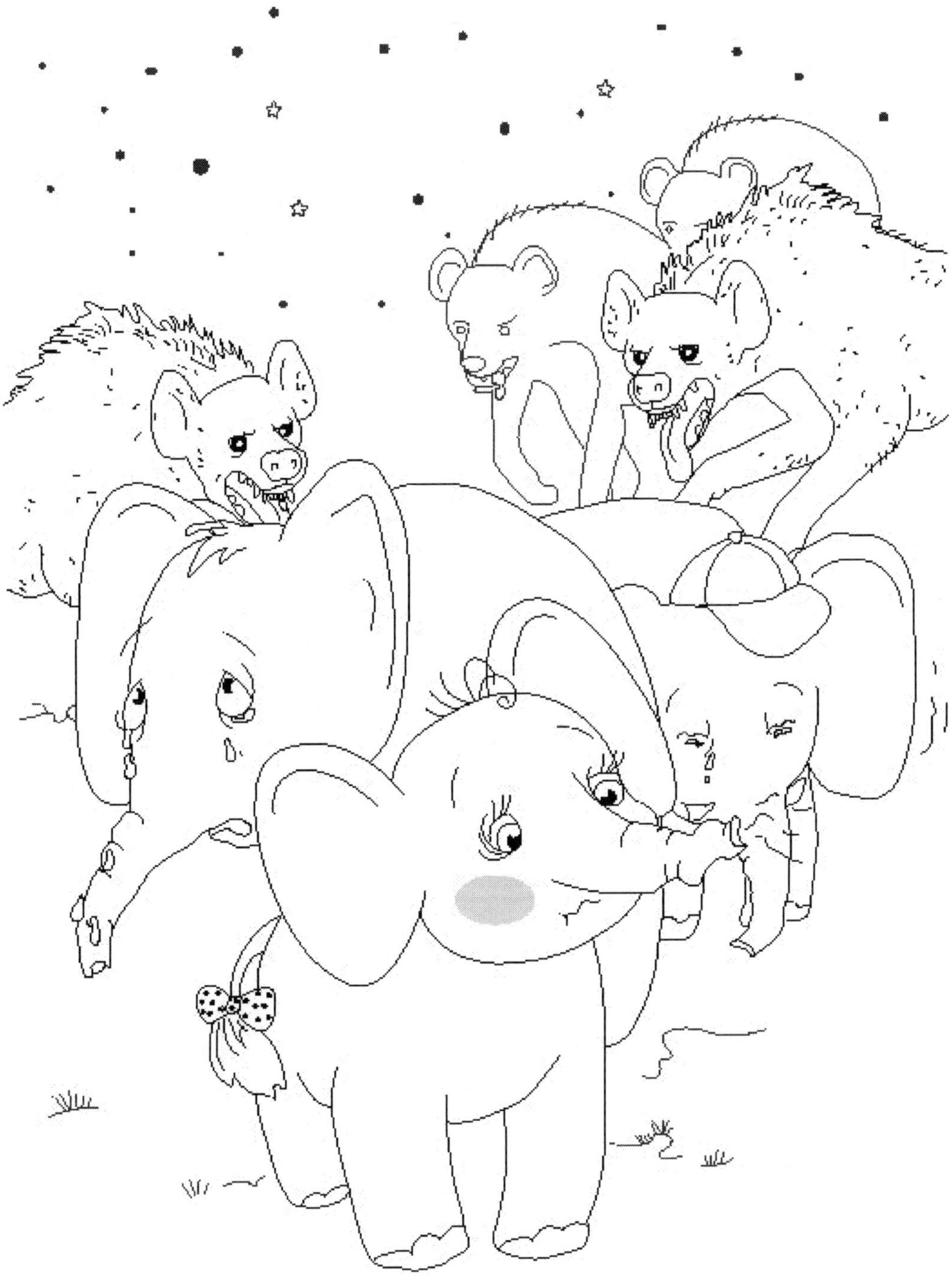

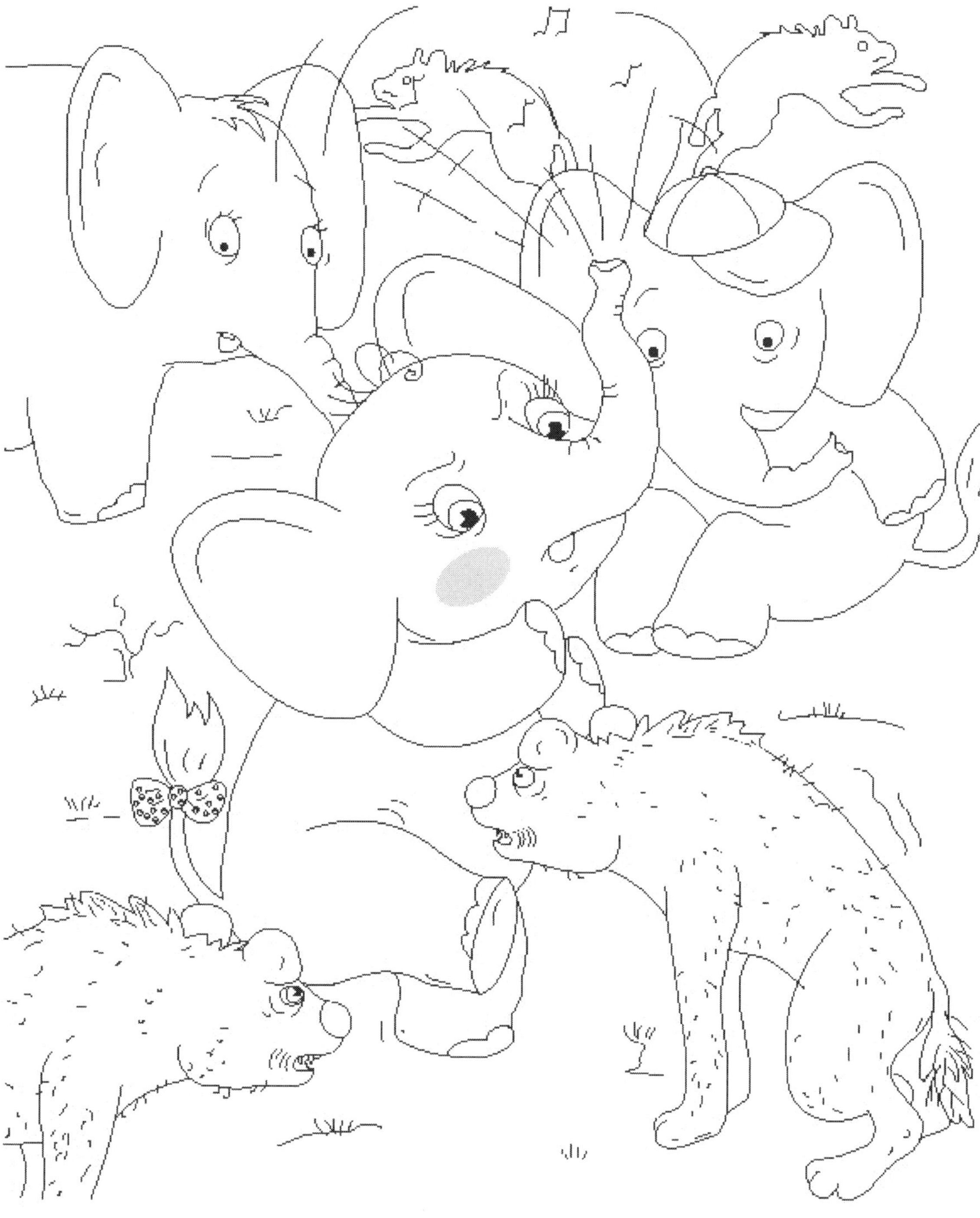

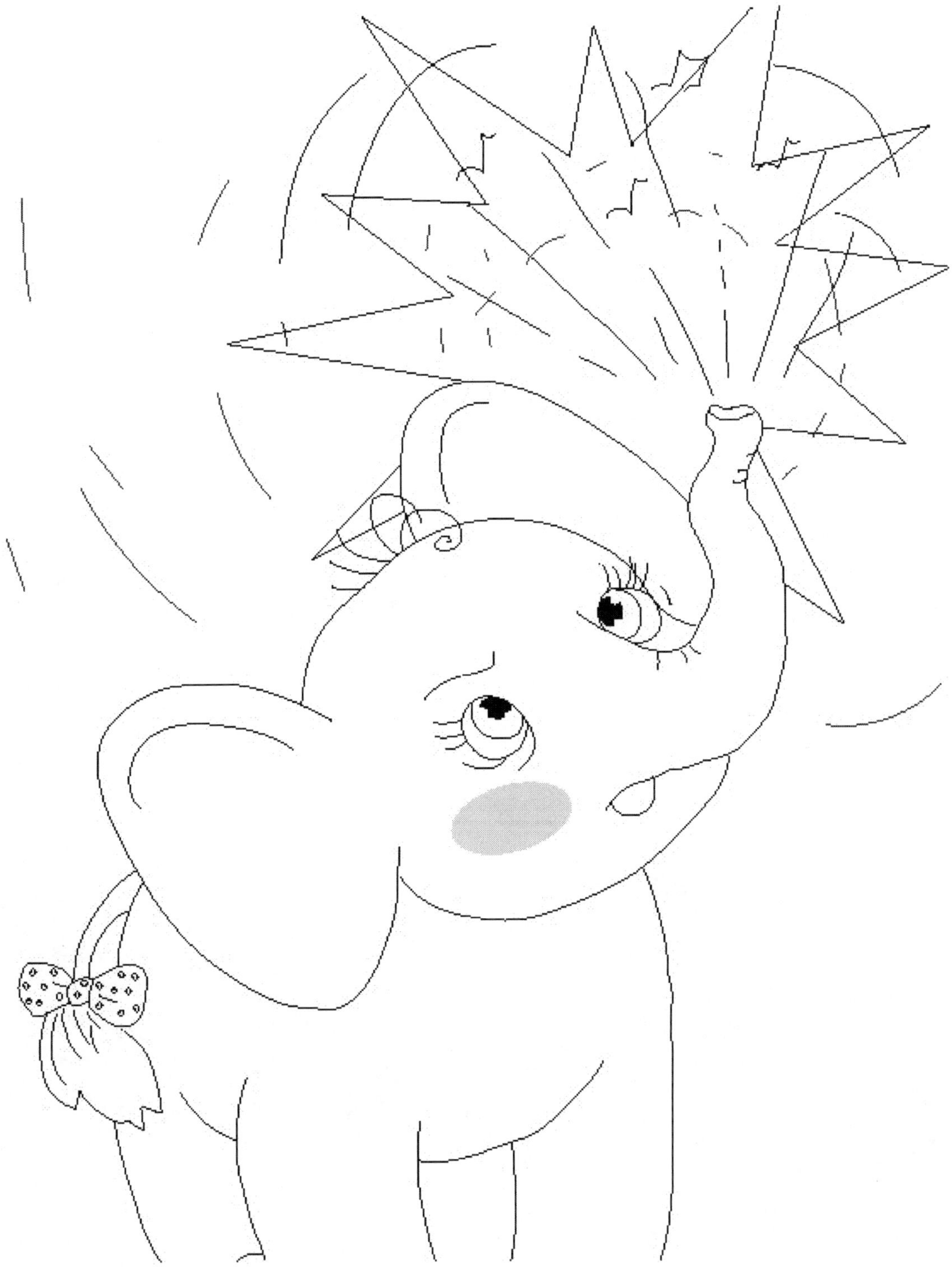

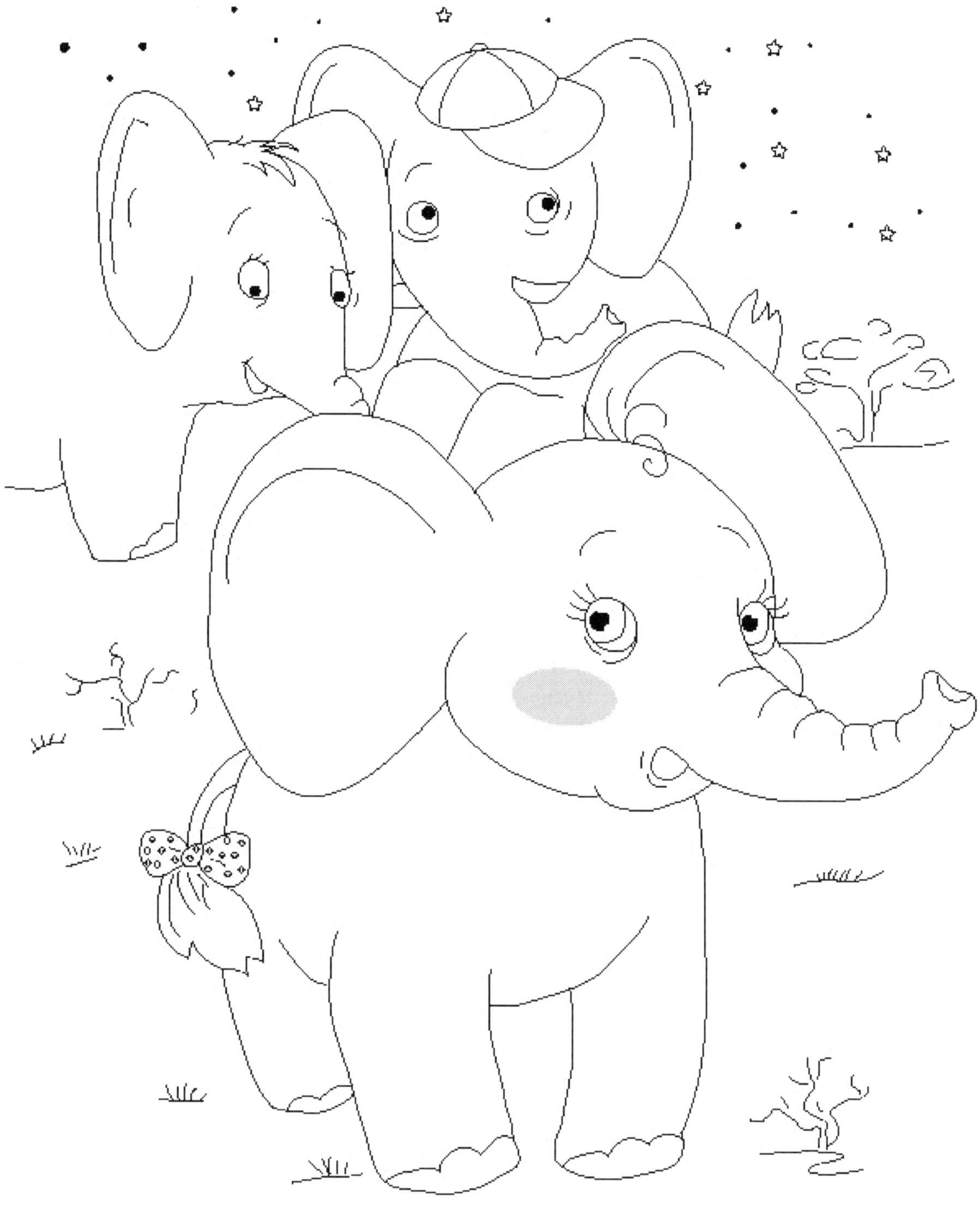

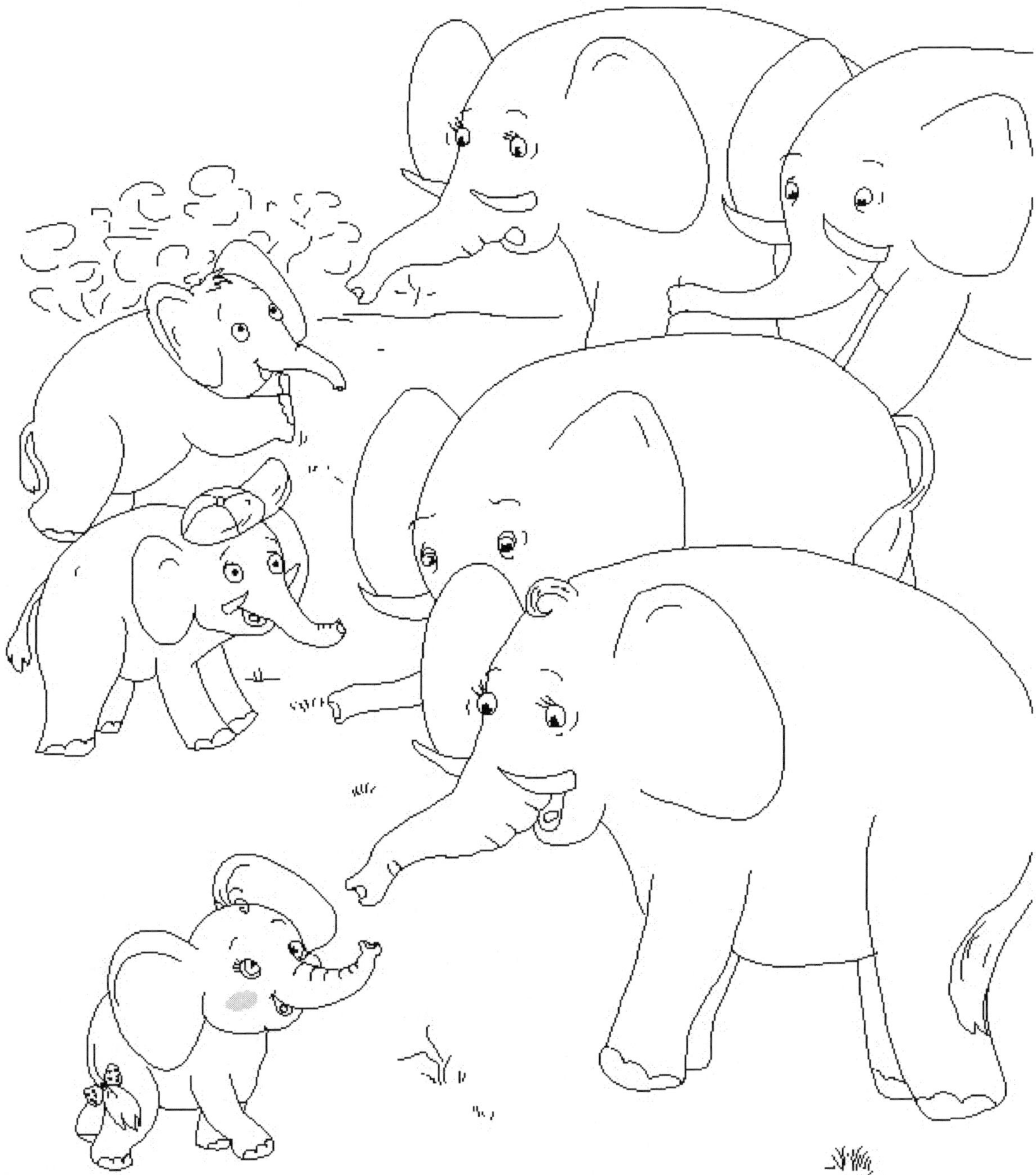

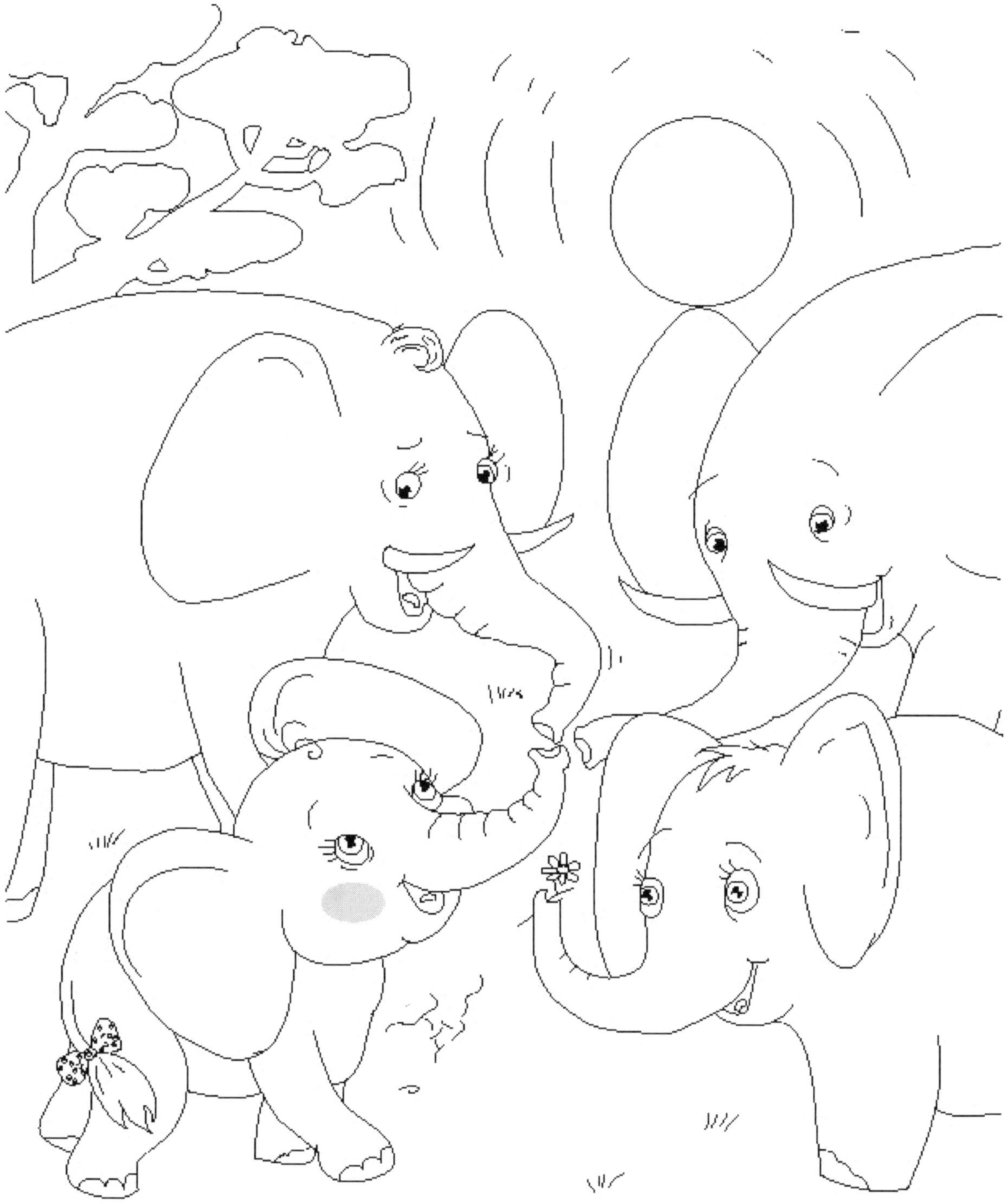

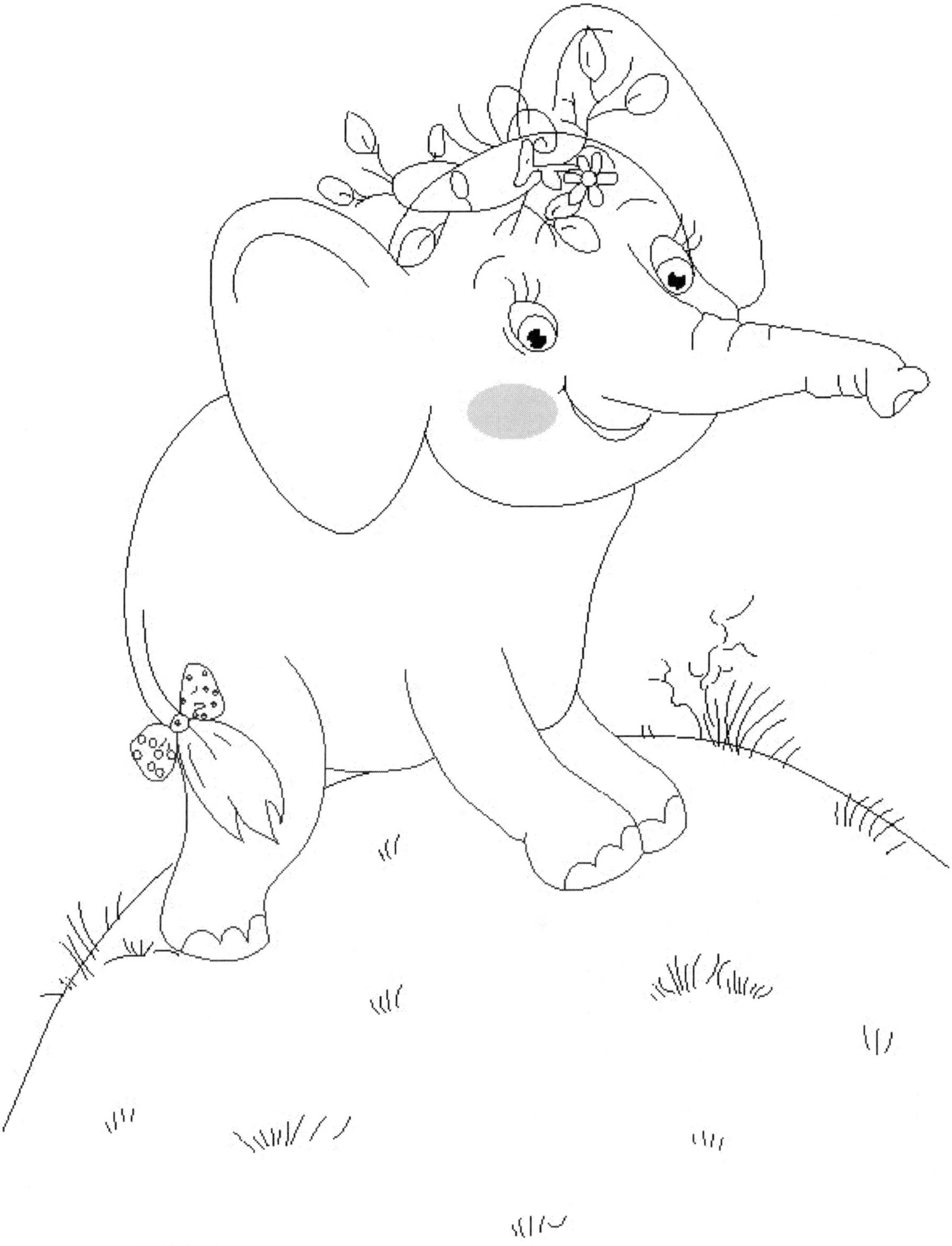

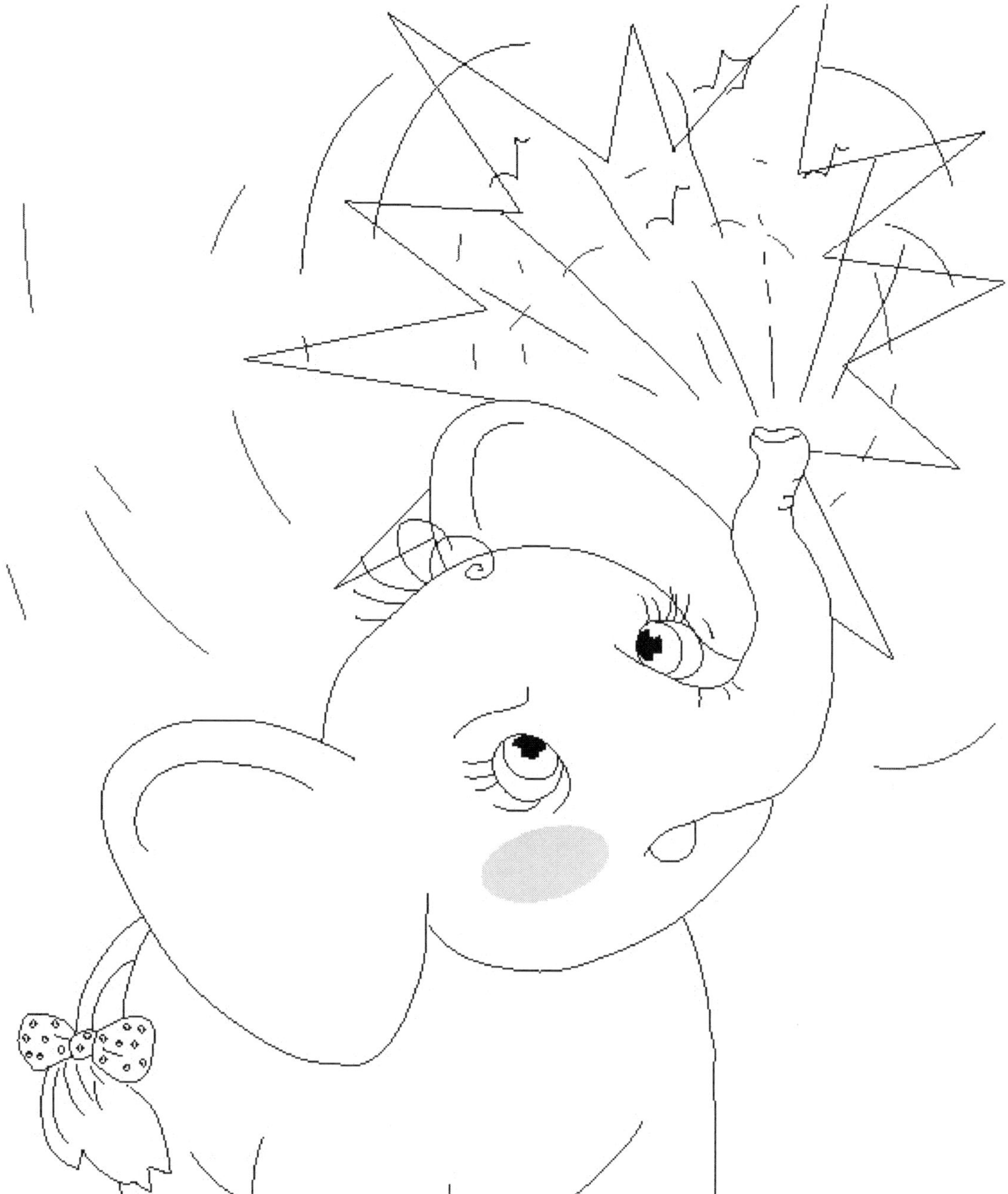

The End!

Made in the USA
Columbia, SC
10 February 2024

31449241R00020